Unstuck: Seven Steps to Break Free and Live Courageously

All Rights Reserved. No portion of this book may be reproduced, stored in a retrieval system or transmitted in any form or by any means (electronic, mechanical, photocopy, recording, scanning or other) except for brief quotations in critical reviews or articles, without the prior written permission of the author and publisher, The Crucible Project.

Published by The Crucible Project
P.O. Box 690894
San Antonio, TX 78269

Library of Congress Cataloging-in-Publication Data

Wooten, Roy D.
The Crucible Project
ISBN: 9798284923627
Imprint: Independently published

Copyright ©2024.
The Crucible Project.
Printed in the United States of America

Dedicated to the 7,400+ men and women who embraced the challenge of becoming "Unstuck" by completing an intensive Crucible Project retreat and experienced radical grace and honesty.

In gratitude for the excellent editing skills of Nancy T. Riley and Judson R. Poling. Thankful for the artwork of John Owen and typesetting of Devra D. Wooten.

Unstuck
Table of Contents

Introduction		1
Step One:	Focus on Who You Are First	7
Step Two:	Don't Do Life Alone	15
Step Three:	Take Responsibility	25
Step Four:	Get Clear on What You Want	31
Step Five:	Step into Accountability	41
Step Six:	Break Free from Shame	47
Step Seven:	Join a Soul Group	53
Crucible Project Resources		59

A Note from the Author

In January 2009 I attended The Crucible Project Men's Retreat because my brother-in law told me that they were doing some incredibly unique things to wake up men. After several decades of reading every book about godly masculinity, attending Promise Keepers, and being a part of at least a dozen more movements for Christ-following men, I seriously doubted there would be anything different at that event.

Boy, was I wrong.

The first thing God showed me was that I had lived my entire Christ-following life believing I was saved but not really having an experiential-level reality of that in my heart. I know experiences and feelings can be fickle, but on the Crucible Project weekend God wonderfully extended my salvation from my head into the deepest recesses of my heart. It felt as if every cell in my body was washed with grace, and I reveled in the new truths he showed me about myself.

That weekend was only the beginning. In the over eighty retreats I have staffed since then, God has helped man after man get unstuck from the things that are holding them back. While most of the 7,300 who have attended one of our retreats are Christ-followers, I have also witnessed God use this ministry to help unbelievers—even those of different religions—experience his grace in surprising ways.

I believe most of what is keeping us from being all that we can be are the barriers that we have imposed upon ourselves. The paradox is that despite our longing for those blocks between God and us to be removed, they were put there by our choosing—and must be lifted by our decisions and actions. That is why I authored this book. It is a collection of stories and reflections meant to help you begin the journey of getting unstuck. It may be work—challenging work—to make the changes you want to make, but you do not have to live shackled to patterns that seem intractable. You have an incredible power God put within you to move through the barriers and break free.

Remember: God is *for* you. He is always good. He loves you and has always been pursuing a relationship with you. His Son, Jesus, our Savior, has made a way for you to connect with God despite your imperfections. He never says, "Get your life right—then come to me." Like the prodigal son's father, he is racing toward you, arms extended, delighted for you to come to him now, just as you are.

This book is not long but it is designed to be read slowly. I suggest you pause after each chapter. Take some time to journal what God is revealing as you go. Talk to God about what he wants to show you as you travel toward breaking free. Read it with a small group or another person you trust and discuss the concepts it touches upon. Make it as personal as you can.

God bless you on your journey!

Roy

Introduction

"For I have the desire to do what is good, but I cannot carry it out. For I do not do the good I want to do, but the evil I do not want to do—this I keep on doing."
—The Apostle Paul

Feeling Stuck

I suppose you could consider it "good news" that you are not the only person who sometimes feels stuck. In Romans, chapter seven, the Apostle Paul describes his own journey of wanting to live a certain way and yet not being able to do so. It really does seem to be a universal human condition.

Sometimes we feel stuck between doing what is right and wrong. But more commonly, we feel stuck trying to make an improvement to our lives that is just not coming easily. For example, we want to eat healthy but instead we keep ordering our favorite comfort foods. We want to take a career leap but fear the unknown. We want to stop an unwanted behavior but find ourselves engaged in it again simply out of habit. We want to improve a relationship but keep falling into the same painful cycles.

What is it like for you when you feel stuck? Maybe you wish you could buy smaller sized clothes, have more money at the end of the month, or get that promotion or job offer. Maybe there are problems in your marriage that you just don't know how to fix or you can't seem to find the time or energy to be the great parent you want to be to your children. Maybe you just want to rest well at night yet sleep eludes you. Perhaps most frustrating, you want a better relationship with God—the one who loves you more than anyone—yet it feels just outside of reach.

According to a recent study, **80% of Americans feel stuck** in their lives. In another study, over 83% of adult Americans report the highest stress levels since the beginning of the 2020 pandemic. Feeling stuck leads to feelings of anxiety, sadness and anger that just makes things worse.

Staying Stuck

Believe it or not, staying stuck *can* have its advantages. There is something comfortable and familiar about staying where we are (even if it feels bad). It may be difficult or painful, but at least we know what we are dealing with. Taking a step toward what we really want is fraught with risks. We do not know what that new reality will be like. We make up a story about the worst things that might happen. If we get what we want, what if the price we pay is to lose something—or someone—precious to us?

Why We Stay Stuck

At the Crucible Project, we observe that for many people, staying stuck appears to cost less than taking the risk to move forward. Even though we say we want something better for ourselves, if we move out of our stuck state, we fear the risk of what else might happen.

For example, if I change my eating habits, I might never have the joy I know I could have from my favorite foods. Or worse, I might make the uncomfortable sacrifices—do everything right—and still not lose the inches that will allow me to wear the smaller sized clothes I want. Or maybe if I have the hard conversation I need to have with my spouse, it leads to a prolonged argument and more discord, not less. Or worse, it might just push them away completely and they finally reach out to that divorce attorney they threatened to call.

We also have observed that part of the reason we stay stuck is that we have ingrained patterns of dealing with stuck situations. Early in life, we reacted to a stuck place with something that worked for us—kept us safe—and it temporarily relieved the tough emotions. Because it worked, we do it again. Now it feels like an automatic pattern that "just happens;" it is part of who we are. How could we possibly give that up?

The poet and philosopher Emily Maroutian puts the problem this way: "You are not stuck. You are just committed to certain patterns of behavior because they helped you in the past. Now those behaviors have become more harmful than helpful. The reason you cannot move forward is because you keep applying an old formula to a new level in your life. Change the formula, to get a different result."

Getting Unstuck

Sometimes we live in the tension of the dilemma that has us stuck and instead of change, we "make our peace" with the suffering.

That is not always a bad thing if we truly cannot make things different. The psalmist wrote, "Why am I so overwrought? Why am I so disturbed? Why can't I just hope in God? Despite all my emotions, I will believe and praise the One who saves me and is my life." (Psalm 42:5 The Voice).

But in so many situations that seem hopeless, there are alternatives. And so we muster what courage we can, and resolve to be done with living stuck. We decide that we are ready to face our fears, take the risk and make the change. We invite God into our fear and go forward anyway.

With help from the Crucible Project retreats, men and women who have courageously decided to face their fears and do "whatever it takes" have found radical changes even beyond what they came to the retreat for. One recent retreat participant said, "Coming out of the retreat I feel transformed. I knew there would be a change, but God has done abundantly more than I could imagine."

Are You Ready to Get Unstuck?

The path toward a new way of being is never walked alone. At the Crucible Project, we believe that getting unstuck happens when we join with others on their journey. Our retreats test and challenge men and women to search beyond surface barriers and break out of the stuck areas in their lives. Then afterward, our small groups led by trained facilitators provide months of support for establishing new patterns and staying unstuck.

At the risk of oversimplifying the process, we have identified seven steps you can take to break free from being stuck. Each one is discussed in the chapters that follow. In time, by consistently applying these principles, you can begin to live the rich and courageous life you were meant to enjoy.

Step One: Focus on Who You Are First

Have you set goals to help you get unstuck only to get bogged down almost as soon you begin? According to several studies, most of us Americans fail to set goals; but when we finally do, a significant percentage give up before new patterns get established. Surely, you have heard (or even experienced) that most New Year's resolutions are usually blown by February.

Start with Who You Are

What if instead of making resolutions, you begin with radically focusing on being who God made you uniquely to be at your core? What if you build on the foundation of the person God made—your true self—and stepped away from striving to be a cardboard cut-out made in the image of what others (or even you) think you should be?

A great place to start is with an intentional effort to give yourself grace and compassion for past mistakes. That will help you come out of the shadows of wearing masks in front of others and instead discover and live from your true self. Begin by being true to who God made you to be. Be kind to the part of you that tried so hard to be accepted by others (and maybe even God). Live from the place of knowing you are already *acceptable* because God says so—even if nobody else says so.

Do Your Internal Messages Line Up with What God Says?

As a Christ-follower, what if you stopped repeating in your head all those critical and judgmental messages that you know are not from God? As you become aware of how you beat yourself up, do what Paul said to do: "Test every message; hold on to what is good, reject every one that is evil (1 Thessalonians 5:22). Then, "..take every thought captive to make it obedient to Christ" (2nd Corinthians 10:5). Check to see if what you are hearing in your mind is truly from God.

Most of us have an internal chatter of which we are not even aware. When we stop to listen to it, we discover it is really quite critical—and blatantly unbiblical. We hear a string of judgments like, "I'm not good enough, I'm a mistake, I don't matter, I'm unlovable, I'm broken, I'm defective, I am not valuable." Is it any wonder with that playing incessantly in the background we are discouraged…and stay stuck?

Yet what does God say is true about you? It is not a mystery—his Word is clear. Read what is there and repeat it aloud to yourself. Embrace it as the core of your identity:

- *I am created in God's image (Genesis 1:27)*
- *I am God's handiwork (Ephesians 2:10)*
- *God breathed life into me (Genesis 2:7)*
- *I am fearfully and wonderfully made (Psalm 139:14)*
- *I am not my own. I was bought at a price (1 Corinthians 6:19-20)*
- *God gave his only son for me (John 3:16)*

- *By grace, I am saved (Ephesians 2:5)*
- *I am redeemed (Ephesians 1:7)*
- *I am justified (Romans 5:1)*
- *I am free from condemnation (Romans 8:1-2)*
- *I am forgiven of all sins (Ephesians 1:7)*
- *I am reconciled to God (Romans 5:10)*
- *I am a new creation (2 Corinthians 5:17)*
- *I have been given a new heart that is good, not evil, and a new spirit has been put in me (Ezekiel 36:26-27)*
- *He has called me out of darkness, into His wonderful light (1 Peter 2:9)*
- *I am blessed by God (Genesis 1:28)*
- *I am crowned with glory and honor (Psalm 8:5)*
- *I am holy and blameless in his sight (Ephesians 1:4)*
- *His grace is lavished upon me (Ephesians 1: 7-8)*
- *I have been given the Spirit of Truth (John 16:13)*
- *I am God's temple and his Spirit lives in me (1 Corinthians 3:16)*
- *I can rest in Jesus Christ (Matthew 11:28)*
- *I am a friend of Jesus Christ (John 15:15)*
- *I am a part of the body of Jesus Christ (1 Corinthians 12:27)*
- *I have every spiritual blessing in Jesus Christ (Ephesians 1:3)*
- *I am complete in Jesus Christ (Colossians 2:9-10)*

- *I am loved (Colossians 3:12)*
- *Nothing can separate me from the love of God (Romans 8:35-39)*
- *His love has been poured out into my heart (Romans 5:5)*
- *I am a citizen of Heaven (Philippians 3:20)*
- *Jesus is preparing a place for me with Him (John 14:3)*
- *I am seated with Christ in the Heavenly realms (Ephesians 2:6)*
- *I have been raised with Christ and now my life is hidden with Christ (Colossians 3:1-3)*
- *I am appointed a witness and servant of Jesus Christ (Acts 26:16)*
- *I am Christ's ambassador (2 Corinthians 5:20)*
- *I am called (Revelation 17:14)*
- *I am chosen and appointed to bear fruit (John 15:16)*
- *I am established, anointed, and sealed by God (2nd Corinthians 1:21-22)*
- *God has a plan for me (Jeremiah 29:11)*
- *He has called me by my name and I am His (Isaiah 43:1)*
- *I am called, justified, and glorified (Romans 8:30)*
- *My calling is holy (2 Timothy 1:9)*
- *I can do all this through Him who gives me strength (Philippians 4:13)*
- *He will never leave me nor forsake me (Deuteronomy 31:6)*

- *I have not been given a spirit of fear, but of power and of love and of a sound mind (2 Timothy 1:7)*
- *I am surrounded by God (Psalm 139:5)*
- *If God is for me, who can be against me? (Romans 8:31)*
- *No one can snatch me from His hand (John 10:29)*
- *I am born of God and the evil one cannot touch me (1 John 5:18)*
- *I am a child of light (Ephesians 5:8)*
- *I am the light of the world (Matthew 5:14)*
- *I received power when the Spirit came upon me (Acts 1:8)*
- *I am a soldier of Jesus Christ (2 Timothy 2:3)*
- *I have been given a living hope (1 Peter 1:3)*
- *He has given me the victory through Jesus (1 Corinthians 15:57)*
- *I am a child of God (John 1:12; Romans 8:16; 1 John 3:2)*
- *I have hope and a future (Jeremiah 29:11)*

What an amazing list of truths! Can you imagine what life would be like with *those* tapes playing nonstop in the background of your mind?

What's Blocking You from Embracing God's Truth?

Now that you are clear on what God says, accepting it as truth may seem risky. Fear can get in the way. It can keep us from letting ourselves believe what God says is true about ourselves.

The challenge is to acknowledge our fears but then move through those limiting beliefs and begin to live from a place of knowing that we are good enough…we have what it takes…we are loved and powerful!

On that note, it may be surprising to discover underneath our fear of failure and self-criticism is a quite different kind of fear. It may not shout as loudly, but it still holds us back. One author describes it this way:

> *"Our deepest fear is not that we are inadequate. Our deepest fear is that we are powerful beyond measure. It is our light, not our darkness that most frightens us. We ask ourselves, 'Who am I to be brilliant, gorgeous, talented, fabulous?' Actually, who are you not to be? You are a child of God. You are playing small does not serve the world. There is nothing enlightened about shrinking so that other people will not feel insecure around you. We are all meant to shine, as children do. We were born to make manifest the glory of God that is within us. It is not just in some of us; it is in everyone. And as we let our own light shine, we unconsciously give other people permission to do the same. As we are liberated from our own fear, our presence automatically liberates others."*
> – Marianne Williamson in *A Return to Love*

Action Step

Let us get practical. A great place to begin is to take a few moments to imagine—or better yet, write out—in detail how your life would be different if you were to live every moment of every day from a place of wellness and belonging. Paint the picture of life based on God being delighted in you. No more striving to be accepted, just an overflow coming from the fullness of embracing all he says is true. Instead of frantically seeking approval and wanting others to validate you, imagine the power and productivity that would result from acting out of the core beliefs that his Word teaches are the unshakable bedrock of our identity.

Who you are not *what you need to do* is the place to begin. But only you can redirect your mind—nobody can think your thoughts for you. You alone do that. It has to start "in here" not "out there." Imagine the reality God made possible in your soul and take every thought captive!

Step Two: Don't Do Life Alone

"Two are better than one because a good return comes when two work together. If one of them falls, the other can help him up. But who will help the pitiful person who falls down alone? And if one person is vulnerable to attack, two can drive the attacker away. As the saying goes, "A rope made of three strands is not quickly broken."
—Ecclesiastes 4:9,10 &12 (VOICE)

Hiding in Isolation

Loneliness will make you sick. Like clinically, physically ill. I am not exaggerating.

A recent study revealed that isolation has detrimental physical and emotional effects. It decreases immune response, exacerbates other illnesses, decreases life satisfaction, contributes to more alcohol and drug abuse, and negatively impacts mental health.

What is driving this trend? Why is something so easy to fix continuing to plague us?

Even though I do not have hard data, I have some fairly good guesses. To begin with, most of us in America can relate to our national ethos of independence and individualism. We want to be self-reliant. We are socialized to value taking responsibility for our well-being. We look down on those who always ask for help, who want hand-outs instead of a hand. We rail against those who are dependent on the "nanny state." But in (rightly) rejecting laziness or leeching off others, we may have overcorrected; the reality is we need for support from time to time, and it is OK to ask for it.

There has been an unintended cost to our quest for self-sufficiency. While we live by the mantra, "I've got to figure it out on my own," we are dying—literally dying—from taking that too far. A former US Surgeon General declared isolation and weak social connections are the most common threat to public health.

Not cancer,
not heart disease,
not diabetes…
loneliness.

Another factor driving this trend is the pain of bad experience. We have all been hurt at one time or another by someone we were close to. We have had a confidence broken or a trust betrayed. Or we look in the mirror and think,

If they really knew _____ about me, they would reject me.

All this makes us struggle to feel safe enough to fully connect with another person. We hide behind surface conversations and pleasantries so that no one really sees us. Our hiding costs us true connection; and we end up isolated and feeling lonely.

Benefits of Connection Outweigh the Risks

At the Crucible Project, we believe that God uses community to heal. God never intended for us to do life alone. We need a group of people to do life with. Everyone needs a safe space where their whole self is welcomed without judgment. To meet that need, the Crucible Project holds retreats, groups, and provides life-coaches "to ignite Christ-like change in men and women through experiences of radical honesty and grace.

According to one report, people who were connected in such an environment had strengthened immune systems, quicker health recovery, lengthened lifespans, lower levels of anxiety and depression, higher self-esteem, greater empathy along with more trust and cooperation.

Staying in isolation may feel familiar, but it is costing you.

There is a different price you pay to move out of isolation into connection: you will have to confront your fear and step out of your comfort zone. But the benefits you get from connecting will be worth the risk of taking off your mask and facing your fear of rejection or judgment.

We Wear the Mask

We wear the mask that grins and lies,
It hides our cheeks and shades our eyes, —
This debt we pay to human guile;
With torn and bleeding hearts we smile
And mouth with myriad subtleties.

Why should the world be over-wise,
In counting all our tears and sighs?

Nay, let them only see us, while
We wear the mask.
We smile, but oh great Christ, our cries
To thee from tortured souls arise.
We sing, but oh the clay is vile
Beneath our feet, and long the mile,
But let the world dream otherwise,
We wear the mask!

—Paul Laurence Dunbar

Stop Wearing a Mask

The poet in the preceding lines captures a universal human reality that comes from our upbringing. In our earliest experiences on earth, we are applauded for some of the things we do while other words or actions receive rejection. The result is that we learn quickly to hide what we truly feel (or want) behind a mask so that people only see the parts of us that get approval. Most humans fine-tune this "skill," so we end up wearing different masks for home, work, church, neighborhood, and friends.

Repeatedly putting on and taking off masks is physically and emotionally exhausting. It has unintended consequences for us and those we love. The incongruence between our actions and our true feelings eventually leads to problems. Our masks can inadvertently slip out of our hands and fall off in an abrupt and destructive way—like a dish dropping on the floor and breaking.

The parts of ourselves we hide behind our masks do not go away. They actually take on a kind of life on their own—and they fight, causing a war within us. Unfortunately, living inauthentically like this not only hurts but it becomes a barrier in our relationship with God and others.

Taking the Mask Off Safely

One of the built-in needs God's placed in our hearts is a longing to be fully seen and fully accepted. True connection can only take place between people who are willing to unmask. We have to come out of hiding and become courageously vulnerable with each other.

At the Crucible Project, we believe that everyone needs a safe place to be real and authentic—to let down our guard and take off all masks. The Apostle Paul said it this way in Ephesians 4:15 (The Message), "God wants us to grow up, to know the whole truth and tell it with love—like Christ in everything."

Do you have a place where "the whole truth" is known and told? Not just truth about God (which is important) but truth about each of us? A place where everyone agrees to be totally authentic, without any mask-wearing?

Emotional Honesty and Openness Leads to Connection

One of the quickest and strongest paths toward true connection begins with self-awareness—knowing and reporting on our own internal emotional climate. Assessing and expressing what is going on inside of me is paradoxically the starting place for connection with what is going on in you. Speaking about my internal emotional state is a way of unmasking and coming out from hiding.

The way to experience deep connection is through courageously communicating my emotional world to another and being open to hearing, without judgment, another person's expression of their internal emotional climate.

Loving God with All Your Heart, Soul, Strength, and Mind

"You shall love, love the Eternal One your God with everything you have: all your heart, all your soul, all your strength, and all your mind; and love your neighbor as yourself."
– Luke 10:27 (The Voice)

In my experience, I find most Christ-followers spend their connection time with God *learning* things—taking in information and thinking about what they discover. Perhaps they express their mind to him—they know how to "love" God mentally—but they haven't experimented with what it means to love God with their heart, strength or soul as well.

In some Christian circles, we are taught to distrust our emotions. While we cannot be ruled by emotions, pretending they do not exist or do not matter is not healthy. At the Crucible Project, we believe that for us to love God with all of who we are, we must discover how to connect with our own emotions and love God in every emotional state. Denying or repressing our emotions is not the answer.

We believe that emotions are a gift from God. We are made in God's image, and he reveals in Scripture he has emotions, too. Jesus expressed a variety of emotions and was without sin: so emotions, in and of themselves, are not sin. The problem is not what we feel, but what we do with what we feel.

Problems with Emotions

Emotions can be problematic. Here are just a few ways we mishandle our emotional world and miss how best to experience them:

- **We are unaware.**
  One of the tough challenges with emotions is that many of us are taught not to have or express some emotions—sometimes in gender-specific ways. For example, it is often socially acceptable for men to express anger but not fear or sadness. Conversely, it is often socially acceptable for women to express sadness but not anger. This is just one example of what contributes to us growing into adulthood without any awareness of what we are truly feeling.

- **We confuse emotions with actions.**
  When we were young, we learned it was more acceptable to hide our emotions. Yet sometimes the only way to get people to respond was to get big and loud. So, we became very confused about how to deal with our varied emotional states. Over the years, our pattern of reacting unconsciously developed into "automatic" behaviors that feels like we have no control over. So, if I feel hurt or sad, I

may try to find a way to numb out—or I express that pain with aggressive language or behavior.

- **We lose control.**
  If we learned not to trust our emotions and ignore them, they do not just go away. So instead of becoming aware and processing our feelings in healthy ways, we end up just reacting—and usually overreacting. We let our feelings run our lives and do not realize how much pain we are causing ourselves (sometimes with legal repercussions). Worse, we hurt those around us and are blind to the damage we are doing. We think if only they would be different, we would be different. But blaming others for our lack of control is never the answer.

There Is a Better Way

Awareness of our emotions opens up a channel for God to give us all the gifts they were meant to provide. We must feel our feelings in order to learn what they might teach us. When we are fully aware of our emotions, we do not have to be ruled by them. We can make choices on purpose—intentionally—instead of reacting. That allows us to move toward becoming more like Jesus.

Awareness of feelings leads to awareness of the choices we are making, which in turn helps us see the consequences of our actions. This knowledge allows us to connect better with those we love. It gives us opportunities to engage with our family, friends, workplace, church, and community from our mature center instead of our immature and emotion-driven self.

Making these improvements requires training and practice. We do not just "decide" to live this way. Becoming more real and dealing more effectively with our emotions is a skill. We need support from others to get better at it. We also need models: not perfect people, but those who are further down the road, who can guide us to our next steps. That is why leaders in the Crucible Project have spent 20 years developing and testing our now proven methods for growth. Our transformational retreats, small groups, and coaching provide men and women opportunities for living powerful, free, and congruent lives.

Step Three: Take Responsibility

The news these days is filled with a variety of upsetting stories: wars and threats of wars, natural disasters, murders, earthquakes, along with ever-increasing political and social divisiveness. Add to that the frequent unexpected life-stressors: the loss of a friend or loved one, financial pressures, career/job/school challenges, relationship struggles, and conflict in the neighborhood or church. It can all feel overwhelming.

What do you do when you feel overwhelmed?

Humans, even Christ-followers, tend to respond to being overwhelmed in predictable ways.

1. **Get Big** - We power up and attempt to take control over anything we can. This can look like "throwing a fit," becoming verbally or physically aggressive, or going off on someone. We do this in person, online, in traffic, behind someone is back and in multiple other ways.

2. **Isolate** - We withdraw from being around others and isolate ourselves. We might think we are seeking solitude—which is typically a good thing—but in fact, we are shirking our responsibilities. This might look like taking too much time away from work, not attending church, avoiding certain relationships, staying in bed all day, or not responding to calls or texts from those depending on us.

3. **Numb Out** – We attempt to stop the feeling of being overwhelmed by simply dulling all our feelings. We abuse

alcohol or other drugs, engage in sexual activities that distract us from pain, binge eat or watch TV to stuff our feelings, or just sleep a lot. Sometimes, our numbing looks much more acceptable, like extreme workouts, or excessive cleaning, or diving deep into a hobby or work rather than actually feel our fear or sadness.

What is Your Avoidance Pattern?

Each one of us tends to respond in a predictable way to feeling overwhelmed. Researchers tell us that our response patterns are set early in life during childhood. When we experienced an overwhelming situation, we tried one or more of the three responses noted above and the one that worked best became our "go-to" strategy.

What somehow gave us a measure of relief as a child may have worked back then, but now we are adults. We usually find those patterns from long ago have outlived their usefulness. In fact, if we are honest, our old ways may actually be costing us with more relationship problems, career challenges, legal issues, or poor health.

Seasons of "Between" are Hard.

Being "between" is an uncomfortable place to find yourself. For example, a job ends, and you find yourself "between" jobs. Maybe a relationship break-up becomes final and you're "between" what you thought you would always have and wondering if there will ever be another you can truly love. Or perhaps you move from a town and community you love to a new city, and you are "between" who and what you've known for so long and who and what is to come.

After the pandemic ended, many of us experienced a "between" season. We lost friends and loved ones, our church changed (or closed), our favorite restaurant or store was gone. But we had not yet established new friends, found a new church, or gotten active as we used to do before it all began. Sometimes, if we *did* try something that we used to enjoy, it somehow felt different, maybe even strange.

God Is in the "Between" Times

What has been gone. What is coming is not here. Our imperfect understanding of the future can create even more anxiety. But if we are open, it is exactly in the "between" times that God can get our attention and do something transformational in us. If we take responsibility for our life, God stands ready to walk with us into a better tomorrow.

In *How to Lead When You Do not know Where You're Going*, Susan Beaumont challenges us to consider a kind of surrender that is not passive but is a great alternative to our constant fruitless striving. She points out that when we fight the reality of any given moment, we may be striving in an unproductive way. Such frenzied thinking and activity, always trying to be somewhere in the future instead of in the present is costly to us. It costs others in our lives, too. We end up spending massive amounts of time and energy that do not pay off, resulting in high levels of fear, sadness or anger.

Surrender, however, provides acceptance of the reality around us. It awakens us to move our energy away from things outside of our control and toward things within our responsibility and power. Surrender means leaving behind and letting go of the right things so that we can welcome the blessings of the moment. Once we surrender in this way, we can discover steps to take responsibility for our future.

Simple Steps to Become a Better You in Your "Between" Times

1. *Invite Christ into your "between" season.* Pray for Him to use your "between" time to reveal anxious thoughts that weigh you down and barriers that hold you back. Open yourself to whatever work He may want to do within you.

2. *Courageously look in the mirror.* Take a deep dive into what is driving you, how life is working (or not working) for you. Notice where you find yourself doing things that are not really you. Acknowledge the ways you numb out and hide or where you shrink back and withdraw. Be prepared to face the unpleasant reality that you might not like what you see.

3. *Do life with others.* God never meant for us to walk alone. Isolation makes us easy targets for the evil one. Find other people also on a journey of growth, who help you create a

safe place where everyone can be real with one another.

4. *Find a trustworthy guide.* The Crucible Project has trained soul-care veterans who have been where you are. Our leaders and coaches have benefitted from our twenty years of deep transformation experiences. Consider reaching out to get resources to help you make the most of you "between" times.

Step Four: Get Clear on What You Want

"You used to turn sticks into swords or dirty flip-flops into glass slippers. You climbed trees and made forts and thought being a doctor wasn't out of reach. Nothing was out of reach. Then somewhere along the way, you lost it."

– John Acuff

What Do You Want for Yourself?

Sometimes what contributes to our being stuck is the gradual giving up on our dreams. Or worse, reality has become so disappointing, we no longer have any dreams left to give up on. *How dare you have a want!* we whisper to ourselves. *Just accept your lot in life—otherwise, you are setting yourself up for disappointment!*

Maybe we lost our wants as we felt the stress of "adulting" while attempting to keep up with our peers. Their path became our path, and we stopped allowing ourselves to be directed by our own desires. Our lofty hopes for a better life faded beneath the weight of bills, job requirements, relational disappointments, and urgent needs of the moment.

Dreaming Again

God built us with the capacity and need to dream. He actually invites us not to copy others, but to look deep within ourselves to find the seeds that are meant to grow into the life we want. In

Psalm 37:4, God promises, "Delight yourself in the Lord and he will give you the desires of your heart." Not somebody else's dream for you—your dream for you. If your heart were full of wicked things, why would God want to give you the desires that reside there?

Proverbs 4:23 says, "Guard over your heart for from it flow the springs of life." God put the springs of life in you, and you need to protect (guard) your deepest desires and longings. You also need to know what those desires are. You have to let yourself dream again to allow them to bubble up—that's one way you access your God-given "living waters."

Dreaming again requires us to be still; to let ourselves be quiet long enough to listen to our soul. We must ask ourselves questions, then pause for the answers to come to us: *How do I want to live my life? What kind of people do I want to do life with? What is my unique design and how does God want me to be a gift to the world?*

"A dream you do not have to fight for is not a dream–it's a nap. One changes your afternoon. The other changes your world."
– John Acuff

A Fresh Start

Once you get more clarity about what you want, it is time to move into action. Effort is required to move beyond where you are now so you can be who you want to be.

While God is obviously sovereign over his creation, he has sovereignly chosen to give us agency. "You have not, because you ask not" (James 4:2) is just one example of not doing our part and consequently missing some blessing God is prepared to give. Proverbs 13:4 has a warning and a promise, "The soul of the sluggard craves and gets nothing, while the soul of the diligent is richly supplied." Note that the sluggard "craves"—he has desires. But he takes no actions.

It may actually feel frightening to have to admit *we reap what we sow*. If we plant nothing, nothing grows. But if we diligently sow and cultivate what we have planted, we will receive a harvest as God blesses us.

Our God-given destiny requires acting on our God-given capacity to participle in his plan. We must "do something" to improve our lives and get unstuck. He will not read our Bibles for us; he will not do acts of kindness we are supposed to do; and he will not give us our dreams if we sit around passively "craving" like the sluggard without acting. Our choices, moment by moment, are moving us either farther away or closer toward our dreams. Our powerful God made us in his image—we are that powerful!

"A well-thought-out plan will work to your advantage…"
                                                        Proverbs 21:5 (The Voice)

Much of the work we do in the Crucible Project helps us increasingly become aware of the choices we are making (or not making) and paying attention to both intended and unintended consequences. That knowledge helps us take full responsibility for what we have created in our lives and moves us toward creating the world we really want.

We must then develop a plan with simple but measurable steps to move us toward our dreams. If that seems overwhelming, we find that making the goals really small—breaking the big strides into manageable steps—enables us to keep moving forward. The goals we give ourselves all have a timeline—a "by when" so we know when we have achieved them. And we typically share those steps with our coach or in our Soul Group, so we get support.

Begin Where You Are

"Without proper self-evaluation, failure is inevitable."
--John Wooden

"There is life all around me, but no life in me." –
-- James Keith Wright

One of the tragic consequences of being stuck is the feeling that life is passing you by. You see others around you appearing to enjoy "life to the full," but you find yourself merely an observer. Others are setting and achieving goals while you feel mired down and unproductive.

You may wonder why…
- You do not have a career, or you feel stuck in an unsatisfactory job
- Your finances remain a challenge year after year.
- You have not completed your educational aspirations.

- You never seem to lose weight or get healthy.
- The relationship you always wanted seems impossible to find.
- You frequently feel distanced from God.

Put More Life in Your Years

There is a popular saying, "It is not the years in your life that count. It is the life in your years." While time may have passed without as much "life" as you want, the good news is *you can begin this minute to put more life into your years.* You do not have to wait on anyone or anything to step into your power and live life abundantly. Your past does not determine your destiny.

YOLO (You Only Live Once)

This popular acronym may be used to justify wanton pleasure-seeking or dangerous risk-taking, but there is another application of it that is much more useful. Because it is true you only live once, let that motivate you to stop wasting your one and only life. Get off the couch. Turn off the show your binge watching. Stop scrolling on social media. Put down your phone. Skip the bar on the way home.

Get into action creating the life you really want. You were made for more—and God is for you!

"You can't go back and change the beginning, but you can start where you are and change the ending."

—C.S. Lewis

Getting Beyond Resolutions

If you made New Year's resolutions this year, you are in good company. According to one report only 35% keep their resolutions and 16% failed to keep any at all. Sadly, even if we write down what we want, something about us gets in the way of achieving those objectives. One study found only 8% of Americans reach their goals *even when they write them down*. With such results, it makes sense that fewer people are making resolutions at all.

If resolutions and written goals do not seem to pay off, where do you even begin?

Assessing Where I Am

"You can't really know where you are going until you know where you have been."
—Maya Angelou

In the soul work we do in the Crucible Project; time is spent doing the important work of honestly assessing where we are. To put it crassly: no more BS. If we do not see the true state of affairs, we may end up majoring on minors and miss the areas that most need our attention.

We find it helpful to assess how we are doing in eight dimensions of our lives to make sure we are not overlooking something important. Those areas are:

- emotional
- physical
- spiritual
- relationships with family
- friendships
- finances
- career
- recreation

If you want help from one of the Crucible Project coaches, you will most likely begin by assessing these areas of your life. Having clarity about "what is" will help you work more effectively toward "what is to come."

We think this failure to self-assess is one of the reasons many resolutions or goal-setting initiatives do not work. For example, say you want to improve your relationship with your spouse. You could decide to invest more time or have a date night. That is a good start. But you may have overlooked the reality that your spiritual life is a mess. Without tending to your soul and your connection to God, you may find trying to make your marriage better lacks a key ingredient for success: a better you.

It could be just the opposite. You want a better relationship with God and so you dedicate time to journal, pray and read your Bible. All well and good. But if you are treating your spouse with contempt and failing to show kindness and grace to your life partner, what makes you think that might not affect your connection with God? The Apostle John warned: "If someone says, 'I love God,' but hates a fellow believer, that person is a liar; for if we do not love people we can see, how can we love God, whom we cannot see? And he has given us this command: Those who love God must also love their fellow believers." (1 John 4:20–21). In 1 Peter 3:7, the Apostle mentions how your prayer life may be adversely affected because you are not tending to important matters in your marriage.

Honest assessment of ALL areas of life will help you see yourself wholistically. Then you can isolate the areas most in need of work. As noted above, you may have to deal with two or even three issues in tandem if you want to make progress in any one of them.

A Crucible Project coach will help you accurately do this self-assessment. You will receive individualized recommendations for resources to help you move toward your goals. As you work on any one area (or several areas), you can check back in with your coach to measure your progress and get encouragement that helps sustain you on the tough but rewarding journey ahead.

Step Five: Step into Accountability

Distracted From Goals

What do you suppose is the attention-span of a goldfish?

I am sure that's never crossed your mind. But I am going to tell you anyway: it's nine seconds.

The reason I share this is because a recent study found that the average human attention span has fallen from 12 seconds (in 2000) to eight seconds—that is less than a goldfish. Is it any wonder we are so easily distracted from achieving the goals we set?

We make a plan, and we resolve its worthy of our best efforts. We tell ourselves this time it is going to work.

But then life happens.

The house needs urgent repair. Your accountant retires and you have to find a new one. A family member becomes ill. Your church goes through a tough leadership transition. A five-year road construction project begins on your daily commute. Reorganization at work means a new supervisor to deal with—or worse, looking for another job. The doctor calls with unexpected news.

"They" Did It to Me

We can find dozens of excuses for why we are off-track meeting our target projections. The distractions of life can ruin the program we put together. We were doing great, until "they" changed something.

"They" are the people we blame when life does not go the way we want it to. "They" make us feel like a victim of circumstances. "They" are the only ones who can do something to make things better.

If only "they" were not getting in the way.

When we feel this way, we must redirect our thought patterns. As author Gary Keller cautions, "When life happens, you can be either the author of your life or the victim of it."

Take Responsibility and Step into Accountability

In the soul work we do through the Crucible Project, we believe that if you do not take responsibility for being the one who must make your life better, you end up living as a victim. In that state of mind, you cannot make the changes you need because you are waiting for someone else to be strong. You give away your power instead of using it. You end up making others accountable, instead of owning your contributions to what is—and, more important, what is going to be.

We believe that even if something is done to us that was not our fault, we can take responsibility to get what we want. We may not be able to control someone else's actions, but we can and must control our reactions.

Taking responsibility for "what happens next" helps us be accountable. Accountability is taking full responsibility for our choices and their consequences. Sometimes, the things we do produce the effects we want. Other times, unintended things happen. We believe we must be accountable for *all* that happens as a result of our actions.

There are many things beyond our control—but when we take responsibility, we regain our agency for what is in our domain. Living with accountability leads to a life with more power to influence our lives.

In his book *The One Thing*, Gary Keller writes, "Taking complete ownership of your outcomes by holding no one but yourself responsible for them is the most powerful thing you can do to drive your success…Accountable people absorb setbacks and keep going…[they] persevere through problems…" Every day we choose one approach or the other, and the consequences follow us forever.

Accountability Leads to Achievement

The tools we use in the Crucible Project—especially our Soul Groups—have enabled people to find remarkable success moving from victim-mode to being accountable and taking responsibility. If you desire to stay on track with your goals regardless of what life throws at you, we believe you need to be accountable. To do that over the long haul, you will need encouragement and support. You will need to have a coach or else be in a group with others who are likewise committed to that level of accountability.

Coaching or being in a Soul Group provides regular connection with others who are willing to be held accountable for their goals and are committed to hold you accountable for yours. Groups provide regular support in a confidential setting for when the unexpected in life happens. They will not take responsibility for your progress, but they will help you do that.

With the stabilizing and empowering influence of a group or coach, you will reach your goals that much quicker. If you want to discuss joining a group or find a coach, check out.
TheCrucibleProject.org.

Step Six: Break Free from Shame

We All Carry Secrets

Everybody has at least one secret. And according to the American Psychological Association, about 97% of people have secrets that trouble them.

According to the same research, people carry on average thirteen secrets that weigh them down. The study found, "The more people's minds wandered to their secrets, the worse off they were." Both guilt and shame are hidden with our secrets, but focusing on shame is especially common.

Guilt vs Shame.

In *Daring Greatly*, researcher Brené Brown distinguishes between guilt and shame. She writes, "guilt is adaptive and helpful—it's holding something we've done or failed to do up against our values and feeling psychological discomfort... shame (is) the intensely painful feeling or experience of believing we are flawed and therefore unworthy love and belonging." Both may feel uncomfortable, but shame is especially harmful to our soul's well-being.

While guilt can help us change when we do something out of line with our better nature, shame tells us we are irreparably broken and unable to change. Guilt says, "You made a mistake." Shame says, "You *are* a mistake."

Shame grows more powerful as we hide the thing that is inconsistent with our values. When we do something wrong, guilt says, "Own what you did. Make amends. Try to make it right." Shame says, "See what a failure you are? Do not let them see you. You must hide."

It is not just what we do to others that causes shame. It can be how we act or think when we are alone. Shame says, "If anyone knew this about you—who you really are—they would run." So, in self-protection, we hide that part of us we think will cause rejection. And then we isolate because we think we are the only one.

The harder we try to solve it—alone—the more shame grows. We fail...then try harder...fail again...try harder again...in a never-ending cycle trying to climb out of an exponentially growing pile of shame. We become more isolated attempting to hide this part of ourselves from others. It ends in broken relationship, depression, legal trouble, hopelessness, anger outbursts, or a lifestyle of engaging in continuous numbing activities.

Carrying Secrets Is Costly

Holding on to a dark secret is costly. It drains us physically and leads to fatigue. Carrying secrets for a long time contributes to low self-esteem, anxiety, depression, and health problems.
We are torn. We want freedom but know it will come at a cost. One study concluded, "...[we] want to confide and get the secret off our chests, but we also want to protect ourselves and our relationships. That conflict is what wears us down."

Letting Light into the Darkness of Shame

Shame is a liar. And like all liars, its power is broken by truth. Shame lives in the shadows, and like all shadow creatures, it cannot withstand light. The antidote for the shameful struggles we wrestle with is to speak those struggles aloud to safe people. James 5:16a (NIV) says, "…confess your sins to one another and pray for each other so that you may be healed." Note the surprising encouragement to tell others about our sins, not just God. Just as confession to others (and God) brings healing from sin, confession to others (and God) helps heal our shame.

We can admit the shame, own the shame and paradoxically get rid of the shame through the single act of sharing the shame. Safe people to whom we reveal what we have been hiding then become God's agents of grace. Shame loses its grip as others enter the space between us and the choke-hold shame has on us.

This act of sharing what weighs us down is not a one-and-done event. Freedom exists as we continually update others on any and every ongoing struggle (in true community, they do the same with us). This kind of openness becomes a lifestyle—and leads us to experience God's Kingdom in ways we may have been missing.

Vulnerability is Strength

Isn't it fascinating that modern psychological research is confirming what God said in the Bible thousands of years ago? Being vulnerable is not weakness—it requires courage to be real. And taking this brave step releases the effects of shame.

Vulnerability = Freedom!

Why is courage needed? Most of us hide—carry secrets—because we want to protect ourselves from the rejection we fear. We must overcome the discomfort that we imagine will follow such disclosure. In truth, opening usually leads to a sense of relief. That is not always the case, but it's still the right thing to do.

Who we share with is important. You cannot just walk into a room; grab the first person you find and start opening about your inner struggles. There are risks involved, and we must understand the potential downside of choosing the wrong person—someone who is not a good listener, or who makes light of our problem, or who tries to fix, or worst of all, betrays confidentiality.

Do your due diligence before you take this crucial step—not everyone can support you well. Sometimes it is good to invest in a professional therapeutic relationship where confidentiality and support are ethically (and legally) demanded.

We Can Help

Within the Crucible Project, we have multiple options to help you. Everything we do flows from our mission: to ignite Christ-like change through experiences of radical honesty and grace. We have over two decades of experience assisting people in making the kinds of changes they only dreamed were possible. A great place to start is through one of our transformational Christ-centered weekend retreats. Check our website for the one nearest you.

If you are not ready to take that step, consider one-on-one personal coaching sessions. The Crucible Project has certified coaches available to help release you from shame. They are trained and skilled facilitators, Christ-followers with high ethical standards, who are committed to help you break free.

Step Seven: Join a Soul Group

"Two are better than one because a good return comes when two work together. If one of them falls, the other can help him up. But who will help the pitiful person who falls down alone?"
—Ecclesiastes 4:9-10 (The Voice)

Why You Need a Soul Group

No matter how tough and independent you think you are or how much you pride yourself on not needing anyone, you were not meant to do life alone. The myth of the self-made, self-reliant person is just that: a myth.

Recall that in the Bible right after God created the first person, he said that it was "not good" for the man to be alone. It was not so much the first man was incomplete without a wife; rather, the man (perfect though he was) needed human companionship. It is still true today: it is not good for us to be alone.

Why do we need other people—why isn't God enough for us?

Strictly speaking, God made us dependent on many things, not just him. People need food, they need sleep, they need to breathe, they need to work—God does not do those things for us, we must do them. That is by design.

It is not that God made us flawed when he made us to need each other; that's how we become fully human. The connection we make with others—and yes, even need—is one way life is enriched. Living in community is also how we fulfill being made in God's image. He is "community": Father, Son, and Holy Spirit. And he made us to be in community as well, to fully demonstrate something profound about who he is.

Bottom line: we need each other.

While a variety of mutual support groups have been around for a long time, over 7,000 men and women have found that the unique processes and leadership provided within the Crucible Project programs have been a catalyst for transformation in their lives.

Among our various offerings are small groups: what we call, Soul Groups. These gatherings are led by Crucible Project trained leaders and use proven Crucible Project processes and curriculum. Many within our community credit their participation in a Soul Group as the most life-transforming work they have ever done.

One recent group member reported, "I have been a part of church small groups, accountability groups and CEO round tables, but nothing has come close to the progress I experienced through my Crucible Soul Group."

You might be asking yourself, *Why should I join a Soul Group?*

Consider the following benefits…

Be Seen and Heard — Joining a Soul Group will provide a regular space for you to share what is going on in your life. Every meeting, your heart will be seen and you will be accepted just as you are.

Get Support in Tough Times — When you are working on yourself, things almost always get harder before they get better. Working in a Soul Group with people you trust gives you the support you need most when things seem the worst.

Exchange Denial for Honesty — You cannot change what you don't see. It often takes others to help us discover our blind spots. Others can also help us peel back layers of denial that keep us pretending things are better than they are. In a Soul Group, you will have the opportunity to not only get honest feedback about how you are being experienced, you will receive grace-filled support to help you break through the barriers that are contributing to your being stuck.

Discover Healthy Relationships — Many of us grew up in dysfunctional homes; we do not even know what trusting, healthy relationships look like. In a Soul Group, Crucible Project leaders provide structure and processes to help you learn what those relationships are like and how to foster them. The training you get in your group will help you positively impact other relationships in your life as well.

Realize Your Growth — In the middle of a journey of transformation, it is often difficult to see progress. We often feel like all the work we are doing isn't paying off. It may also be that those closest to us—who have withstood the worst of our sharp edges—find it hard to trust that the work we are doing is making substantial and lasting change. But those in your Soul Group can see the changes you make and will help you celebrate and encourage even the slightest movement in the right direction.

Grow in Your Relationship with God — In a Soul Group, you will likely discover things about you that are getting in the way of your relationship with God. Those barriers are often less obvious than the behaviors and patterns everyone sees. In your Soul Group you can work on those unseen problems while you also make changes in the things that you and everyone around you are aware of.

Support and Serve Others — Growth in community is rarely a one-way process. We cannot just be takers; we need to be givers as well. We often discover surprising growth happens in us when we help others deal with the problems they are facing. Being a part of a Soul Group gives you opportunities to both give and receive support and encouragement.

Take What You Learn to Your Home, Church, and Work — Gains made in your Soul Group diffuse throughout all your relational world. Any time you experience transformational growth, you acquire new tools to also connect with your family, support your local church community and improve your team at work.

Crucible Project Resources

Here again are the Seven Steps to help you get unstuck in life:
- STEP 1: Focus on Who You Are First
- STEP 2: Do not Do Life Alone
- STEP 3: Take Responsibility
- STEP 4: Get Clear on What You Want
- STEP 5: Step into Accountability
- STEP 6: Break Free from Shame
- STEP 7: Join a Soul Group

Many of us know how heartbreaking it is to be bound by behaviors, thought patterns and forces that seem unconquerable. But while the Crucible Project is not the only place you can find resources to help you, we want you to be aware of just how much we offer.

If you want to accelerate your growth and get unstuck, we are here to assist you on that journey.

Free Materials
Blog

Much wisdom has been gathered over the years and is available for you in the Crucible Project's blog. Search for the topic you are seeking advice on or scroll through hundreds of blog articles written by a variety of authors including pastors, counselors, coaches, business entrepreneurs and community leaders. TheCrucibleProject.org/blog

Free Materials
Podcast

Subscribe to The Crucible Project Podcast to receive a weekly drop of the latest interview. Guests include many of the international cadre of 24 Crucible retreat leaders. You will also hear from other authors, coaches, counselors, pastors, and business leaders. TheCrucibleProject.org/podcast

Free Materials
Weekly Compass Resource

Would you like a weekly note of encouragement to help keep you headed in the right direction? Every week a new resource for your journey is delivered to your inbox. Subscribe at the bottom of our main web page. TheCrucibleProject.org

Free Materials
The Crucible Project Website

Visit our website at TheCrucibleProject.org to learn more about how we can help you get unstuck and become the person you want to be. Watch testimonial videos of leaders like you who have broken free and are now living with integrity, passion, and courage, fulfilling their God-given purpose. If you have any questions, want to have a discussion about groups, retreats or about any of our other resources please reach out to The Crucible Project at: Communications@TheCrucibleProject.org.

Offerings
Men's and Women's Weekend Retreats

Our flagship transformational initial Men and Women's Retreats test and challenge participants to search beyond superficial "answers" or cosmetic adjustments to uncover hidden barriers to their progress. Only through discovering the root cause of our problems—often a pattern that goes all the way back to childhood—can we break out of the stuck areas in our lives. Our retreats are a unique opportunity for you to totally disconnect from life "out there," leave behind distractions from electronic devices, and take a deep dive into becoming the person you believe God wants you to be. We are happy to share that 98% of Crucible Project Retreat attendees report they "got all they came for"—and many add, "I got even more than I hoped for!" The initial Weekend Retreat also provides deep connection with others so that you do not have to do life alone any longer.

TheCrucibleProject.org/crucible-weekend-for-women
TheCrucibleProject.org/crucible-weekend-for-men

**Offerings
Online Groups**

Discovery groups are small circles of either men or women (typically 6-10) who are committed to grow into deeper levels of authenticity, honesty, transparency, and grace. They do so in a safe, non-condemning online environment. Groups typically meet three times monthly and are led by a Crucible Certified facilitator. A monthly fee is a part of the group commitment. TheCrucibleProject.org/soul-groups

What you can expect:

- Support and positive challenge for your continued journey and the goals you most want to reach.
- Learning from the deepest experience of others as they share their personal soul work with you.
- An unparalleled group experience of safety, openness, and trust
- Tools, skills, and healing to live a more passionate, powerful and intentional life.

Offerings
Coaching

If you are not ready for a group or a weekend yet, coaching with The Crucible Project may be an alternative to help you grow. We offer coaching services designed to help you identify your goals and develop a plan to achieve them. Our coaches are experienced and trained to provide you with the support and guidance you need to succeed.

TheCrucibleProject.org/coaching

Here are just a few benefits of coaching with The Crucible Project:

1. Clarity
   One of the main benefits of coaching is that it helps you gain clarity about your goals and aspirations. Our coaches will work with you to identify what you truly want in life and help you develop a plan to achieve it.

2. Accountability
   Another benefit of coaching is that it provides you with accountability. Our coaches will help you set realistic goals and hold you accountable for achieving them. This can be

incredibly motivating and help you stay on track even when things get tough.

3. Support
Change can be difficult, but with coaching from The Crucible Project, you do not have to go it alone. Our coaches are there to support you every step of the way, providing encouragement and guidance when you need it most.

4. Personal Growth
Coaching is not just about achieving your goals; it is also about personal growth. Our coaches will help you identify areas where you can grow and develop, both personally and professionally.

5. Lasting Results
Finally, coaching with The Crucible Project can help you achieve lasting results. By working with our coaches, you'll develop the tools and strategies you need to succeed long after your coaching sessions are over.

Speaking Presentations and Podcasts — If you are looking for a speaker at your upcoming event or a guest on your podcast and would like to book a Crucible leader, reach out to us at Unstuck@TheCrucibleProject.org with your event details.

Support the Crucible ministry – The Crucible Project is a 501c3 non-profit ministry. Donations made to the Crucible Project are eligible for IRS deductions according to law. If you would like to join the movement by financially supporting the ministry you can make a secure online donation at TheCrucibleProject.com

Made in the USA
Coppell, TX
02 March 2026